NATURAL GAITS

Pierre Alferi

NATURAL GAITS

*translated from the French
by Cole Swensen*

LOS ANGELES
SUN & MOON PRESS
1995

Sun & Moon Press
A Program of The Contemporary Arts Educational Project, Inc.
a nonprofit corporation
6026 Wilshire Boulevard, Los Angeles, California 90036

This edition first published in paperback in 1995 by Sun & Moon Press
10 9 8 7 6 5 4 3 2 1
FIRST SUN & MOON EDITION
©1991 by Pierre Alferi
Published originally as *Les Allures naturelles* (Paris: P.O.L., 1991)
English language translation ©1995 by Cole Swensen
Published by permission of P.O.L.
Biographical material ©1995 by Sun & Moon Press
All rights reserved

This book was made possible, in part, through an operational grant from the
Andrew W. Mellon Foundation and through contributions to
The Contemporary Arts Educational Project, Inc.,
a nonprofit corporation

Cover: Thomas Eakins, *Man Walking*
Cover Design: Katie Messborn
Typography: Guy Bennett

LIBRARY OF CONGRESS CATALOGING IN PUBLICATION DATA
Alferi, Pierre
[Allures naturelles. English]
Natural Gaits / Pierre Alferi; translated from the French by Cole Swensen
p. cm — (Sun & Moon Classics: 95)
ISBN: 1-55713-231-3
I. Swensen, Cole, 1955. II. Title. III. Series
PQ2661.L437A78513 1995
841'.914—dc20
95-21104
CIP

Printed in the United States of America on acid-free paper.

Without limiting the rights under copyright reserved here, no part of this
publication may be reproduced, stored in or introduced into a retrieval
system, or transmitted, in any form or by any means (electronic, mechanical,
photocopying, recording or otherwise), without the prior written permission
of both the copyright owner and the above publisher of the book.

CONTENTS

I pressure 7
II dissipation 12
III inertia 16
IV circulation 20
V condensation 23
VI drift 24
VII transmission 26
VIII fall 30
IX oscillation 34
X recoil 39

I

1. pressure
   can double the pressure
   acting on a supple body
   laterally, vertically—headed down headed
   up—and from the heart to the skin maintain
   the voluminous appearance (the buoy) pressure
   can triple more deeply equally divided can quadruple
   without a trace the movements
   astonishingly easy, light, not
   owned not knowing the idea alone
   disturbs the idea of the tension
   of the fragility of arteries
   and tissues and causes
   a vague
   reticence.

2   how the background insists
    still on the unleashed form, through
    minute decisions, numerous,
    implicit: by conceiving of things
    —their equally shared constraint—
    not to be said, not to be done
    be it deaf, abstract
    the swimmer's stroke imagined
    from the point of view
    of the molecules of displaced water.

3   a peripheral feeling appears
after a few months hardly
a feeling rather
an easement (a buffer zone) an adjacent
street, empty. One could view
what follows as a progressive
shrinking each child
was several the place
was not missing the number
decreased slowly the oldest
ones so compacted
they could no longer breathe.

4   it appears that bubbles
wander free
as air, even
in the compressed column
of a fire hose.

5   but the depth tattoos itself on the back
    the body fights against itself for space
    underwater *to skim the bottom* says something:
    this particular abrasion acting slowly
    on the species was at first a visceral fight and
    formed the flattened fish of the uncharted depths
    their eyes protruding their chests crushed their translucent
    fins in the image of a human
    body, hydrocephalic and without organs
    limbs atrophied except for the hands
    of the body in working or swimming order
    as it through kinesthesia
    and the converging of sensations
    toward two or three foci
    sees itself.

II

1. like smells and heat, sound
propagates itself but more abstractly
freely and more quickly consuming
the presence of each
thing it inscribes itself most
tenuously. No
material, no image
even one deaf or very soft
when struck in the right place
would not give off sound but sounds
extorted from these things
that have made a vow of silence
by drumming on the corner
of a table by scraping along a fence with
a pencil as one puffs on a
dandelion are pure
products of dissipation for the
pure pleasure of hearing them
say nothing.

2   a box-shaped appliance
    that makes no noise
    no part of which can be seen to move
    pierced by small holes to which one can
    hold up a hand and feel nothing
    that one forgets to unplug unless
    one has forgotten to plug it in
    is a household
    humidifier.

3   the improvisationists (accomplished
    casual) contrapuntally attack
    against a sparse background (undulating
    ambiguity of space and music-stand
    a net of chords rent
    in places or whose weave has been enlarged
    by escape) the phrase
    which will dash up the harmonics
    four at a time (their jazz
    a dissipated chant their chorus
    a solo).

4   ...the drop follows
    its course when emotion
    runs dry, waylaid...*the words have spoken out
    of turn:* empty territory
    hair and nails of the dead...

    all heat consumes its source
    smoke fades the wax
    perspiration dissolves the body's edge

    . . . .
    a voice its throat
    disorder carries it off

    . . . .
    where it's all the same

    . . .
    entropy

III

1. when nothing gathers nothing
   occurs beyond inertia
   occasions waves gathering in its wake
   nothing but a nothing that nonetheless
   gets in the way and the slightest contact
   inverts the direction of flight (unaware
   that across two windows he is watched, a stranger
   dresses, undresses, sits, rises, picks up, puts down
   the receiver): first the chaos
   of particles in suspension
   then the full-stop. A common gesture
   video-taped
   a gesture sampled over itself
   superimposed in all directions like
   a breakdance step whose position is no more
   than the inverse of its inverse, is already
   something else: an object
   crystallized unmoved.

2   unlike the kaleidoscope
    which juggles shards
    of tinted glass, the thaumascope
    paves its field with hexagons
    by cutting from each a triangle
    that it reverses
    flipping it over onto each of its sides.
    A section unfolding
    whose edges become axes
    of symmetry.

3   once speed falls below a certain point
    equilibrium is disrupted. The sound of the coin
    rolling on its edge, wobbling, showing heads
    or tails, beginning to spin
    sound that hesitates concentric sound
    that concentrates and gives up
    is recognized among many as the
    gasp of the needle when the arm
    slides toward the center and the record
    stops. Then
    it does no good to start it up
    again but rest the head and arm to watch
    the contagion spread
    striking all that moves—unbreakable bodies
    of silent films (flickering
    of images, indolence
    of the soundtrack).

4   movement without hindrance
    is a state (half solid—
    the same comings and goings
    in the same place plate it
    polish it) and what remains,
    a pavement.

IV

1 it's a matter of reclaimed
   verve and a rhythmic
   breath that acts on the hand
   that acts on the eye that acts on the mind
   that acts on the hand (feed-back) rotation
   and constant linear motion an even
   seam or even millefeuille dough stretched
   folded—interleaved—
   so it comes and so
   it goes to the end
   of the rolling pin if there's a rolling pin
   there.

2   with heavy traffic
    comes a foreign rhythm
    almost an arrangement of planes
    in suspension or vanishing
    within the frame   you could say
    one a well-lit room   two a window
    three a street just beyond   four a wrought-iron
    fence   five a row of sycamores   and
    between and among these lace-work screens
    men & women   passing
    a single time in a straight line
    hats & coats   a sleight of hand
    feeds a deck of punch cards
    swallowed & resurfacing without trace
    the keys of a player piano.

3 an image less clear
than its background: a face turning
the movement of a face, its image stopped
extracted, to face
the glance as it is landing but not
the landed glance, the path of a glance sweeping
the arc of a circle, one does not yet know
if it is landing. The image taken
from circulation revives it
needs renewal and like it
demands that various moves, both straight
and arced, involved in a single stroke, combine to
describe it. This image
is the image retained.

V

The blank stare
arrested
—clearer
sharper—by a wall
blind and blank where the shadow
deepens and its circle
shrinks. So small
but so clear, so sharp.

VI

1 less than a chord, accord
   is a potential of every
   pitch, as is boredom or waiting,
   of every sensation: instead of
   reconciling several it interpolates
   each one elsewhere; though sometimes
   so far behind the melody
   (drifting, derived
   sampled) that it sounds odd
   if not false, though one senses that enthusiasm
   no more than distaste, the gracious blend
   of all that one senses can't
   place it: in constant discord
   with nothing, this nothing which, after all
   exists and comes through it all unscathed.

2 how much more unsettling the silent
   game of the continental plates;
   the path—one imagines it as
   erratic indeed—of the
   planet; to know, to not
   know that things don't follow
   their own; or if they do
   that we are definitely (satellite
   freed) in no position
   to say so.

VII

to S.D.

1 speeding along the rails the glance grasps something; from
this something natural perspective emanates folding & refolding
a fan which contains
things whose names come too late to fit the description each
focal plane
simultaneously translates itself against the slower rhythm of the
following
plane which serves as a reference, such as:
—unfurling   series   posts, trees, girders
— —marching   individuals men, cars, buildings
— — —pivoting   masses   hills, spires, outskirts
— — — — fixed   backdrop   clouds, night (pierced
by sun, moon)
the whole thing sliding, a perfect crossing of *homo viator*
perfectly legible except for the bumps, the muffled
sound of the axles, such as:
break everything   break   everything break   everything

2   the aerial metro:
    two
    series of growing Ns
    mirrored meet in one
    x.

3   or in a car approaching a field
    of wheat—of corn—of cross-hatchings which form
    a mass—stain—chaos when
    the lines of flight between
    the planted rows (the simplest
    figure imposed) suddenly
    appear, then disappear, a knot
    which splays: a reading in which
    clarity
    is not a matter of depth
    and analysis but of speed
    and angle.

4   for it is not the *end*
of life but what's on either
side. The child's game
of walking on the very edge of the sidewalk
spreading his arms when needed
or using his hands as vertical visors
surrounded by peril
emerges much later to imagine
when we say *return to nothingness*
a simple derailing the sense
of the word *delirious*
for example a draft horse
who has been blanketed
and fitted with blinders
and yet (in the roadway) shies.

VIII

1   in case of attack or stroke one naturally assumes
the cause to be the fall which was only the effect
                                              —always deaf
always dark this sound, except when it happens to come from
    [water always
so saddening—
        for it better illustrates
the case the   accident
        (unfair) (unforseen)
than does a   rupture
        (unreal) (unrecorded)
of a vessel. It seems more true, this that
weighs
        for example among those out for a walk, the one
who lags behind, feeling the *weight of existence?*
                                                that
weight which proves and prevents it, physical, under which
it will be so easy, one day, to break down once
and for all having only run up
against something
        and this

across which one falls
                        and all
that occurs by chance, isolated, this
or that: less avoidable, more accidental, as true
as the primary movement of primary matter.

2 nothing falls but
   rain (snow, hail) and sometimes
   leaves. The rest
   slides or
   staggers.

3   how we miss the steps of
sleep knocking—head-
first—
against a floor lower than the floor,
harder, then another even lower, even
harder.

IX

1   all repetition becomes
>   enjoyable, to the degree that it weakens
> reflex requires, restlessly regular
>   as a clock, a stronger push
> toward sleep and dream. Thus the intoxication
>   by mouth, vein or exchange of
> bodily fluids, of these (bad)
>   habits wherein lie
> imbalance and symmetry: one is
>   free(r) by giving up freedom
> and these motions that finish
>   beyond the body, natural
> gaits or violent caresses
>   (those high-strung, mechanical
> which *lower us to the level of beasts*)
>   are more worthy than others
> of a soul—are animal motions.

2   to think *yes* while shaking
     N O with the head
     then to nod Y E S while thinking
     no makes the neck swerve
     strangely in its twist.

3   since walking   rowing
    chewing scratching brushing your hair   your teeth
    fornicating reading writing as well as various tics   spasms
    reproduce the teeth of the saw of the encephalogram
    so that a mechanism in itself reversible   impeccable
    makes one forget
    as does the pendulum of a grandfather clock
    what it measures in a straight line and that nothing real
    finds itself there twice.

4   the flickering of anything
when glimpsed
when it's tuned-in precisely
fascinates, which is to say
lulls to sleep.

5   rather than erratic leaps
oscillation: inversion
of the chord (but each
simple insoluble mood
forgets all the others—not their effects
their becoming (except
for that always latent mood
so clear that it would leave nothing
in a latent state and would put
an end to oscillation (but
the chord not matched
to its own becoming
resolves nothing.

X

1 perhaps the recoiling movement that precedes and prolongs
a gesture of aggression, that following a ball
in water makes a wave that pushes it away or when air
is disturbed and the bright speck of dust dances
when approached by a hand, becoming for the amoeba
reflex and for the snail's horns, retractable
claws, could impose itself like a
character trait if true discretion
didn't erase those traits in the process of increasing
distance.

2   for a toy car
    to meet is to spring forward
    is to crash is to throw it in
    reverse to pivot to spring again.

    sid dulen

to E.H. & O.C.

3   a hole in the middle of the vaulted ceiling
    produces, when the bronze door is opened,
    a rush of air into this *beautiful monument*
    which takes us *so far back*—
    nowhere—pure return, incessant, neither of
    nor to, rather a beautiful overturning, since
    that which it commemorated, it has
    eclipsed or at least converted
    in the upheaval on the day of its inauguration
    and the inscription that bears witness—i.e.
    witness to a forgetting and to a series
    of reappropriations—as each phrase read
    for the first time, the head
    bent back, barely deciphering,
    makes the tongue recoil.

4   the yellow capsules of the
    balsam flower (noli-me-tangere
    & impatiens), (evasion
    & abandon) when we touch
    them explode.

5   when one thinks of it an instant
doubles. The striking
of this storm is the *striking
of this storm* but only the second
formed a memorable event (when present
it was already receding: you wondered
if you'd really seen it, if you hadn't
already seen somewhere the *striking
of this storm*). For the second
detaches from the background of an hour
of changing weather is the instant of which
one thought, thinking
make it return.

PIERRE ALFERI

Born in Paris, where he now lives and works, Pierre Alferi has published two book-length philosophical essays, *Guillaume d'Ockham, le singulier* (1989) and *Chercher une phrase* (1991), and three books of poetry, *Les Allures naturelles* (1991), *Le Chemin familier du poisson combatif* (1992) and *Kub Or* (1994). American translations of his work have appeared in *Série d'écriture, Tyuonyi: The Violence of the White Page, Avec*, and *Exact Change Yearbook*. With Suzanne Doppelt, Alferi is the co-founder of the magazine *Détail*.

SUN & MOON CLASSICS

This publication was made possible, in part, through an operational grant from the Andrew W. Mellon Foundation and through contributions from the following individuals and organizations:

Tom Ahern (Foster, Rhode Island)
Charles Altieri (Seattle, Washington)
John Arden (Galway, Ireland)
Paul Auster (Brooklyn, New York)
Jesse Huntley Ausubel (New York, New York)
Luigi Ballerini (Los Angeles, California)
Dennis Barone (West Hartford, Connecticut)
Jonathan Baumbach (Brooklyn, New York)
Roberto Bedoya (Los Angeles, California)
Guy Bennett (Los Angeles, California)
Bill Berkson (Bolinas, California)
Steve Benson (Berkeley, California)
Charles Bernstein and Susan Bee (New York, New York)
Dorothy Bilik (Silver Spring, Maryland)
Alain Bosquet (Paris, France)
In Memoriam: John Cage
In Memoriam: Camilo José Cela
Bill Corbett (Boston, Massachusetts)
Robert Crosson (Los Angeles, California)
Tina Darragh and P. Inman (Greenbelt, Maryland)
Fielding Dawson (New York, New York)
Christopher Dewdney (Toronto, Canada)
Larry Deyah (New York, New York)
Arkadii Dragomoschenko (St. Petersburg, Russia)
George Economou (Norman, Oklahoma)
Richard Elman (Stony Brook, New York)
Kenward Elmslie (Calais, Vermont)
Elaine Equi and Jerome Sala (New York, New York)
Lawrence Ferlinghetti (San Francisco, California)
Richard Foreman (New York, New York)
Howard N. Fox (Los Angeles, California)
Jerry Fox (Aventura, Florida)
In Memoriam: Rose Fox
Melvyn Freilicher (San Diego, California)
Miro Gavran (Zagreb, Croatia)
Allen Ginsberg (New York, New York)

Peter Glassgold (Brooklyn, New York)
Barbara Guest (Berkeley, California)
Perla and Amiram V. Karney (Bel Air, California)
Václav Havel (Prague, The Czech Republic)
Lyn Hejinian (Berkeley, California)
Fanny Howe (La Jolla, California)
Harold Jaffe (San Diego, California)
Ira S. Jaffe (Albuquerque, New Mexico)
Ruth Prawer Jhabvala (New York, New York)
Pierre Joris (Albany, New York)
Alex Katz (New York, New York)
Tom LaFarge (New York, New York)
Mary Jane Lafferty (Los Angeles, California)
Michael Lally (Santa Monica, California)
Norman Lavers (Jonesboro, Arkansas)
Jerome Lawrence (Malibu, California)
Stacey Levine (Seattle, Washington)
Herbert Lust (Greenwich, Connecticut)
Norman MacAffee (New York, New York)
Rosemary Macchiavelli (Washington, DC)
In Memoriam: Mary McCarthy
Harry Mulisch (Amsterdam, The Netherlands)
Iris Murdoch (Oxford, England)
Martin Nakell (Los Angeles, California)
In Memoriam: bpNichol
NORLA (Norwegian Literature Abroad) (Oslo, Norway)
Claes Oldenburg (New York, New York)
Toby Olson (Philadelphia, Pennsylvania)
Maggie O'Sullivan (Hebden Bridge, England)
Rochelle Owens (Norman, Oklahoma)
Bart Parker (Providence, Rhode Island)
Marjorie and Joseph Perloff (Pacific Palisades, California)
Dennis Phillips (Los Angeles, California)
Carl Rakosi (San Francisco, California)
Tom Raworth (Cambridge, England)
David Reed (New York, New York)
Ishmael Reed (Oakland, California)
Tom Roberdeau (Los Angeles, California)
Janet Rodney (Santa Fe, New Mexico)
Joe Ross (Washington, DC)
Jerome and Diane Rothenberg (Encinitas, California)
Edward Ruscha (Los Angeles, California)

Dr. Marvin and Ruth Sackner (Miami Beach, Florida)
Floyd Salas (Berkeley, California)
Tom Savage (New York, New York)
Leslie Scalapino (Oakland, California)
James Sherry (New York, New York)
Aaron Shurin (San Francisco, California)
Charles Simic (Strafford, New Hampshire)
Gilbert Sorrentino (Stanford, California)
Catharine R. Stimpson (Staten Island, New York)
John Taggart (Newburg, Pennsylvania)
Nathaniel Tarn (Tesuque, New Mexico)
Fiona Templeton (New York, New York)
Mitch Tuchman (Los Angeles, California)
Paul Vangelisti (Los Angeles, California)
Vita Brevis Foundation (Antwerp, Belgium)
Hannah Walker and Ceacil Eisner (Orlando, Florida)
Wendy Walker (New York, New York)
Anne Walter (Carnac, France)
Jeffery Weinstein (New York, New York)
Mac Wellman (Brooklyn, New York)
Arnold Wesker (Hay on Wye, England)

If you would like to be a contributor to this series, please send your tax-deductible contribution to The Contemporary Arts Educational Project, Inc., a non-profit corporation, 6026 Wilshire Boulevard, Los Angeles, California 90036.

SUN & MOON CLASSICS

AUTHOR	TITLE
Alferi, Pierre	*Natural Gaits* 95 ($10.95)
Antin, David	*Selected Poems: 1963–1973* 10 ($12.95)
Barnes, Djuna	*At the Roots of the Stars: The Short Plays* 53 ($12.95)
	The Book of Repulsive Women 59 ($6.95)
	Collected Stories 110 ($24.95) (cloth)
	Interviews 86 ($13.95)
	New York 5 ($12.95)
	Smoke and Other Early Stories 2 ($10.95)
Bernstein, Charles	*Content's Dream: Essays 1975–1984* 49 ($14.95)
	Dark City 48 ($11.95)
	Rough Trades 14 ($10.95)
Bjørneboe, Jens	*The Bird Lovers* 43 ($9.95)
du Bouchet, André	*Where Heat Looms* 87 ($11.95)
Breton, André	*Arcanum 17* 51 ($12.95)
	Earthlight 26 ($12.95)
Bromige, David	*The Harbormaster of Hong Kong* 32 ($10.95)
Butts, Mary	*Scenes from the Life of Cleopatra* 72 ($13.95)
Cadiot, Olivier	*L'Art Poetic* 98 ($10.95)
Celan, Paul	*Breathturn* 74 ($12.95)
Coolidge, Clark	*The Crystal Text* 99 ($11.95)
	Own Face 39 ($10.95)
	The Rova Improvisations 34 ($11.95)
Copioli, Rosita	*The Blazing Lights of the Sun* 84 ($11.95)
De Angelis, Milo	*Finite Intuition* 65 ($11.95)

DiPalma, Ray	*Numbers and Tempers: Selected Early Poems* 24 (11.95)
von Doderer, Heimito	*The Demons* 13 ($29.95)
	Every Man a Murderer 66 ($14.95)
Donoso, José	*Hell Has No Limits* 101 ($12.95)
Dragomoschenko, Arkadii	*Description* 9 ($11.95)
	Xenia 29 ($12.95)
Eça de Queiroz, José Maria de	*The City and the Mountains* 108 ($12.95)
Federman, Raymond	*Smiles on Washington Square* 60 ($10.95)
Firbank, Ronald	*Santal* 58 ($7.95)
Fourcade, Dominique	*Click-Rose* 94 ($10.95)
	Xbo 35 ($9.95)
Freud, Sigmund	*Delusion and Dream in* Gradiva 38 ($13.95)
Gilliams, Maurice	*Elias, or The Struggle with the Nightingales* 79 ($12.95)
Giraudon, Liliane	*Pallaksch, Pallaksch* 61 ($12.95)
	Fur 114 ($12.95)
Giuliani, Alfredo, ed	*I Novissimi* 55 ($14.95)
Greenwald, Ted	*The Licorice Chronicles* 97 ($12.95)
Guest, Barbara	*Defensive Rapture* 30 ($11.95)
Hamsun, Knut	*Victoria* 69 ($10.95)
	Wayfarers 88 ($13.95)
Hansen, Martin A.	*The Liar* 111 ($12.95)
Hardy, Thomas	*Jude the Obscure* 77 ($12.95)
Haugen, Paal-Helge	*Wintering with the Light* 107 ($11.95)
Hauser, Marianne	*Me & My Mom* 36 ($9.95)
	Prince Ishmael 4 ($11.95)
Hawkes, John	*The Owl* and *The Goose on the Grave* 67 ($12.95)
Hejinian, Lyn	*The Cell* 21 ($11.95)
	The Cold of Poetry 42 ($12.95)
	My Life 11 ($9.95)

Hoel, Sigurd	*The Road to the World's End* 75 ($13.95)
Howe, Fanny	*Radical Love* 82 ($21.95, cloth)
	The Deep North 15 ($9.95)
	Saving History 27 ($12.95)
Howe, Susan	*The Europe of Trusts* 7 ($10.95)
Jackson, Laura (Riding)	*Lives of Wives* 71 ($12.95)
James, Henry	*What Maisie Knew* 80 ($12.95)
Jenkin, Len	*Careless Love* 54 ($9.95)
	Dark Ride and Other Plays 22 ($13.95)
Jensen, Wilhelm	*Gradiva* 38 ($13.95)
Jones, Jeffrey M.	*Love Trouble* 78 ($9.95)
Katz, Steve	*43 Fictions* 18 ($12.95)
Larbaud, Valery	*Childish Things* 19 ($13.95)
Lins, Osman	*Nine, Novena* 104 ($13.95
Mac Low, Jackson	*Pieces O' Six* 17 ($11.95)
Marinetti, F. T.	*Let's Murder the Moonshine: Selected Writings* 12 ($12.95)
	The Untameables 28 ($11.95)
Messerli, Douglas, ed.	*50: A Celebration of Sun & Moon Classics* 50 ($13.95)
	From the Other Side of the Century: A New American Poetry 1960–1990 47 ($29.95)
Morley, Christopher	*Thunder on the Left* 68 ($12.95)
Nerval, Gérard de	*Aurélia* 103 ($12.95)
Novarina, Valère	*The Theater of the Ears* 85 ($13.95)
North, Charles	*Shooting for Line: New and Selected Poems* 102 ($12.95)
Propertius, Sextus	*Charm* 89 ($11.95)
Queneau, Raymond	*The Children of Claye* 92 ($13.95)
Rakosi, Carl	*Poems 1923–1941* 64 ($12.95)
Raworth, Tom	*Eternal Sections* 23 ($9.95)
Romero, Norberto Luis	*The Arrival of Autumn in Constantinople* 105 ($12.95)

Rosselli, Amelia	*War Variations* 81 ($11.95)
Rothenberg, Jerome	*Gematria* 45 ($11.95)
Sarduy, Severo	*From Cuba with a Song* 52 ($10.95)
Scalapino, Leslie	*Defoe* 46 ($11.95)
Schnitzler, Arthur	*Dream Story* 6 ($11.95)
	Lieutenant Gustl 37 ($9.95)
Steppling, John	*Sea of Cortez and Other Plays* 96 ($14.95)
Sorrentino, Gilbert	*The Orangery* 91 ($10.95)
Stein, Gertrude	*How to Write* 83 ($13.95)
	Mrs. Reynolds 1 ($11.95)
	Stanzas in Meditation 44 ($11.95)
	Tender Buttons 8 ($9.95)
Steiner, Giuseppe	*Drawn States of Mind* 63 ($8.95)
Streuvels, Stijn	*The Flaxfield* 3 ($11.95)
Svevo, Italo	*As a Man Grows Older* 25 ($12.95)
Taggart, John	*Loop* 150 ($11.95)
Thénon, Susana	*distancias / distances* 40 ($10.95)
Van Ostaijen, Paul	*The First Book of Schmoll* 109 ($10.95)
Van Vechten, Carl	*Parties* 31 ($13.95)
Vesaas, Tarjei	*The Ice Palace* 16 ($11.95)
Waldrop, Keith	*Light While There Is Light: An American History* 33 ($13.95)
Walker, Wendy	*The Sea-Rabbit or, The Artist of Life* 57 ($12.95)
	The Secret Service 20 ($13.95)
	Stories Out of Omarie 56 ($12.95)
Wellman, Mac	*Two Plays: A Murder of Crows and The Hyacinth Macaw* 62 ($11.95)
Wieners, John	*The Journal of John Wieners / is to be / called* 106 ($12.95)
Wilde, Oscar	*Salome* 90 ($9.95)
Zola, Emile	*The Belly of Paris* 70 ($14.95)